1/02
DW

Sojourner Truth

Abolitionist, Suffragist, and Preacher

Colonial Leaders

Lord Baltimore
English Politician and Colonist

Benjamin Banneker
American Mathematician and Astronomer

Sir William Berkeley
Governor of Virginia

William Bradford
Governor of Plymouth Colony

Jonathan Edwards
Colonial Religious Leader

Benjamin Franklin
American Statesman, Scientist, and Writer

Anne Hutchinson
Religious Leader

Cotton Mather
Author, Clergyman, and Scholar

Increase Mather
Clergyman and Scholar

James Oglethorpe
Humanitarian and Soldier

William Penn
Founder of Democracy

Sir Walter Raleigh
English Explorer and Author

Caesar Rodney
American Patriot

John Smith
English Explorer and Colonist

Miles Standish
Plymouth Colony Leader

Peter Stuyvesant
Dutch Military Leader

George Whitefield
Clergyman and Scholar

Roger Williams
Founder of Rhode Island

John Winthrop
Politician and Statesman

John Peter Zenger
Free Press Advocate

Revolutionary War Leaders

John Adams
Second U.S. President

Ethan Allen
Revolutionary Hero

Benedict Arnold
Traitor to the Cause

King George III
English Monarch

Nathanael Greene
Military Leader

Nathan Hale
Revolutionary Hero

Alexander Hamilton
First U.S. Secretary of the Treasury

John Hancock
President of the Continental Congress

Patrick Henry
American Statesman and Speaker

John Jay
First Chief Justice of the Supreme Court

Thomas Jefferson
Author of the Declaration of Independence

John Paul Jones
Father of the U.S. Navy

Lafayette
French Freedom Fighter

James Madison
Father of the Constitution

Francis Marion
The Swamp Fox

James Monroe
American Statesman

Thomas Paine
Political Writer

Paul Revere
American Patriot

Betsy Ross
American Patriot

George Washington
First U.S. President

Famous Figures of the Civil War Era

Jefferson Davis
Confederate President

Frederick Douglass
Abolitionist and Author

Ulysses S. Grant
Military Leader and President

Stonewall Jackson
Confederate General

Robert E. Lee
Confederate General

Abraham Lincoln
Civil War President

William Sherman
Union General

Harriet Beecher Stowe
Author of Uncle Tom's Cabin

Sojourner Truth
Abolitionist, Suffragist, and Preacher

Harriet Tubman
Leader of the Underground Railroad

Sojourner Truth

Abolitionist, Suffragist, and Preacher

Norma Jean Lutz

Arthur M. Schlesinger, jr.
Senior Consulting Editor

Chelsea House Publishers

Philadelphia

Produced by 21st Century Publishing and Communications, Inc.
New York, NY. http://www.21cpc.com

CHELSEA HOUSE PUBLISHERS
Production Manager Pamela Loos
Art Director Sara Davis
Director of Photography Judy L. Hasday
Managing Editor James D. Gallagher
Senior Production Editor J. Christopher Higgins

Staff for *SOJOURNER TRUTH*
Project Editor Anne Hill
Associate Art Director Takeshi Takahashi
Series Design Keith Trego

The Chelsea House World Wide Web address is
http://www.chelseahouse.com

First Printing
1 3 5 7 9 8 6 4 2

Library of Congress Cataloging-in-Publication Data

Lutz, Norma Jean.
     Sojourner Truth / Norma Jean Lutz.
         p.   cm. — (Famous figures of the Civil War era)
     Includes bibliographical references and index.
     ISBN 0-7910-6007-1 — ISBN 0-7910-6145-0 (pbk.)
         1. Truth, Sojourner, d. 1883—Juvenile literature. 2. Afro-American
abolitionists—Biography—Juvenile literature. 3. Afro-American women—
Biography—Juvenile literature. 4. Abolitionists—United States—Biography—
Juvenile literature.   5. Social reformers—United States—Biography—
Juvenile literature. [1. Truth, Sojourner, d. 1883. 2. Abolitionists. 3. Reformers.
4. Afro-Americans—Biography. 5. Women—Biography.]   I. Title. II. Series.

E185.97.T8 L88 2000
305.5'67'092—dc21   00-038403
[B]   CIP

Publisher's Note: In Colonial, Revolutionary War, and Civil War Era
America, there were no standard rules for spelling, punctuation,
capitalization, or grammar. Some of the quotations that appear in
the Colonial Leaders, Revolutionary War Leaders, and Famous
Figures of the Civil War Era series come from original documents
and letters written during this time in history. Original quotations
reflect writing inconsistencies of the period.

Contents

This is a view of the Catskill Mountains near the birthplace of Sojourner Truth. Born into slavery, young Isabella, as Sojourner was then known, lived in terrible conditions.

"Now the War Begun"

When thinking of slaves, slave owners, and plantations, we usually picture the southern United States before the Civil War. However, in the late 18th century, slaves were bought and sold in New England as well. As early as 1626, Dutch settlers in a colony named New Netherlands imported blacks from Africa to work on their farms.

Years later the British bought the area from the Dutch, renamed it New York, and began to import even more slaves. Although their numbers were fewer than in the South, slaves were still considered important to the economy.

In Ulster County, New York, in the town of Hurley, about 80 miles north of New York City, lived one of those slave owners. Colonel Johannes Hardenbergh, a wealthy grist mill operator, owned a large parcel of land within sight of the Catskill Mountains between the Hudson and Delaware Rivers.

Two of Hardenbergh's slaves, James and Betsey, had faithfully served Hardenbergh for many years. James was known as Baumfree, which means "tree" in **Low Dutch**. He earned the name because, as a young man, he stood straight and tall as a tree. Betsey, a large stocky woman, was called Mau Mau Bett, an affectionate Low Dutch term for mama or mother.

This older couple had borne 10 or 12 children, all of whom had been sold away by their master. In approximately 1797, Mau Mau Bett gave birth to a girl whom the master named Isabella. Her parents nicknamed her Belle. No one recorded Belle's birth, and she was not even given a last name. She was known simply as

Isabella's parents may have looked like this couple. They were very sad that all their children were sold away by their master.

Hardenbergh's Belle. One day, she would choose her very own name—Sojourner Truth. (The word **sojourner** means "one who travels.")

Although most descendants of the Dutch settlers spoke English in public, they spoke only Low Dutch at home, especially to their slaves. Being ignorant of English kept the slaves from learning more than their masters wanted them to know about the world around them. Isabella grew up speaking only Dutch.

When this slave girl was a toddler, Mr. Hardenbergh died. His son Charles inherited the estate, which included the slaves. Charles built a large building to use as a hotel, and moved his slaves from their cabins into the basement of this hotel.

The basement's floor was loosely constructed, allowing the dampness to arise from the muddy foundation. All the slaves slept together on the loose boards on the floor. Sojourner remembered this period of her life in her biography:

> She shudders even now, as she goes back in memory, and revisits this cellar and sees its inmates, of both sexes and all ages, sleeping on those damp boards, like the horse, with a little straw and a blanket.

A few years after Isabella's birth, Mau Mau Bett had one more child, a son named Peter. Isabella was pleased to have a younger brother to love, but her mother knew it was just one more child who might be taken away from her arms.

Isabella knew little about her older siblings. But she heard a great deal about Michael and Nancy, the two just older than she and Peter. They had been taken away fairly recently, and the pain was still fresh in her mother's heart.

Mau Mau Bett told how a large **sleigh** pulled up to the Hardenbergh home. Curious and excited, five-year-old Michael ran to get a closer look. When he saw men locking his three-year-old sister, Nancy, into a sleigh box, he realized they were being taken away. Like a frightened deer, he bolted into the house and hid under a bed. The hiding did no good. The men dragged him out, loaded him on the sleigh, and drove away. The grief Mau Mau Bett still carried was deep and heavy. She would never see them again.

When she was nine, Isabella was sold at a slave market like this one. Her new master beat her regularly.

The story frightened Belle, making her wonder if one day she too would be carted away. What would she do without the love and protection of Mau Mau Bett and Baumfree? Mau Mau Bett did her best to comfort her children by telling them about a loving God who lived in the sky. "[W]hen you are beaten, or cruelly treated, or fall into any trouble, you must ask help of him, and he will always hear and help you." Mau Mau Bett taught young Isabella and Peter to kneel down and repeat the Lord's Prayer. She told them never to lie or steal, and always to obey their masters.

Sometimes Isabella would hear her mother groan aloud. When she asked the reason, Mau Mau Bett would tell how her heart ached for all her lost children. Pointing to the stars, she would tell young Isabella and Peter, "Those are the same stars, and that is the same moon, that look down upon your brothers and sisters, and which they see as they look up at them, though they are ever so far away from us, and each other."

When Isabella turned nine, the lawmakers in the state of New York were arguing about how to get rid of, or **abolish**, slavery. Some felt it should be abolished all at once; others said it should be done gradually. Some felt that owners should be paid for their slaves. Others said no, free all the slaves with no payment to the owners. While they argued, thousands of slaves continued to suffer under the cruel **bondage**.

The situation at the Hardenbergh estate changed suddenly when Charles died. The entire estate was up for auction, including slaves. It was certain that Isabella and Peter would be sold, but what would become of old Baumfree if his faithful wife were sold away? The Hardenbergh family made the decision to save trouble by giving Mau Mau Bett her freedom.

At first that sounded like good news, but where could this elderly couple go? They asked to remain in the basement of the Hardenbergh house, but they had to make their own living, which would be nearly impossible.

Meanwhile, the slave auction was terrifying —especially for nine-year-old Isabella. Unable to understand a word of English, she could only guess what was happening. When it came time for Isabella to stand on the auction block, all eyes were on her. The gavel came down hard, and when the auctioneer shouted "Sold," Isabella became the property of a man named John Neely (some references spell his name "Nealy"). Neely had paid $100 for one slave girl, with a flock of sheep thrown in for good measure.

As Isabella stated in her biography, "Now the war begun!"

When she was a teenager, Isabella was sold to a master who lived in a small New York town like this one. The cold winters were hard because Isabella didn't have warm clothes or shoes.

Serving Many Masters

John Neely and his wife were English-speaking storekeepers from Kingston's Landing. While John could understand Dutch, his wife could not. The Neelys' store had not been doing well, and Mrs. Neely blamed the Dutch people in the area for their problems. She then took out her anger on Isabella.

Since neither could understand the other, Isabella did not know what Mrs. Neely told her to do. If she was sent to fetch one thing, she would bring back something totally different. Mrs. Neely showed no patience or kindness. Each time her anger flared, she beat the girl. Isabella described it as being like a war.

Because she didn't have warm enough clothing, the cold New York winters were misery for Isabella. Without shoes, the little girl's feet were never warm. There was plenty of food in the Neely home, but while Isabella was fed well, she was beaten often.

One day, when Isabella was only 11, Mrs. Neely sent her to the barn. There Mr. Neely was waiting for her. He had heated a bundle of rods over hot embers. Tying her hands in front of her, he began to beat her bare back with the heated rods.

Screaming from the pain, she at last fainted, falling into the straw and into a pool of her own blood. The trauma of this childhood beating never left her. As an adult Isabella would say, "And now when I hear 'hem tell of whipping women on the bare flesh, it makes *my* flesh crawl, and my very hair rise on my head!" From then on she determined to do anything possible to avoid another cruel beating.

Shortly after she had arrived at the Neely home, Isabella heard that her mother had died.

The girl was brokenhearted, thinking of all the love Mau Mau Bett had given her. Isabella began praying very hard that her father would come and protect her from the mean-spirited Neelys. From what little Mau Mau Bett had told her, she knew that God answered prayers.

To her great joy, Baumfree did come. The two had a tearful reunion. Because Baumfree was filled with grief at being left all alone, Isabella said nothing about her own pain. But as they walked out to the gate to say goodbye, somehow the truth was revealed. Perhaps he placed his hand on her back and she flinched from pain. Her mistreatment greatly saddened the old man. Isabella asked her father to please find her a new owner, and he promised to do what he could.

Each day, the little girl returned to their parting spot and reminded God of her prayer for a better master. In a short while, a fisherman by the name of Martin Schryver came by. He and his wife lived on a farm only five miles from the Neelys. They also owned and operated a tavern.

Like the slaves pictured here, Isabella worked in the fields for her new owners. She worked very hard to please her new master.

No doubt he had been sent by Baumfree. Mr. Schryver purchased Isabella and took her away.

The Schryvers were uneducated, but they were not cruel. Isabella remembered the awful beating from Mr. Neely and determined she would work doubly hard. Without the threat of Mrs. Neely's whippings, Isabella quickly learned

English from people who came in and out of the tavern. Throughout her life, she would speak English with a strong Dutch accent.

Working for the Schryvers, Isabella was expected to unload heavy catches of fish, plant and hoe the corn, gather woodland roots and herbs from which beer was made, and work in the tavern. Her hard work was rewarded with warm clothing, food, and a roof over her head. From the rowdy customers at the tavern, Isabella learned to curse and smoke a pipe. She would later be able to stop the cursing, but the pipe habit stayed with her for many years.

Isabella also learned about the world around her from conversations in the

Sojourner picked up the habit of smoking a small white clay pipe when she was young. After becoming a Christian, she believed that using tobacco was wrong but was unable to break her habit. A friend once commented to her that the Bible says no unclean thing will enter the kingdom of heaven, adding that a smoker's breath is unclean. To which Sojourner quipped that, when she went to heaven, she would be leaving her breath behind.

In later years, her friends finally convinced her to give up smoking.

tavern. To her surprise, she learned that not all black people were slaves. She began to think about being free from slavery. If she were free, she could go straight to her father and take care of him in his old age.

But before that wonderful freedom could be hers, she received the bitter news: Baumfree had died. After the death of Mau Mau Bett, Baumfree lived with two other elderly freed slaves in a small cabin. None of them had the ability to find work or to provide for themselves. Eventually the two companions died. Later, Baumfree was found all alone in the cabin, frozen to death.

With her parents both gone and her little brother sold, Isabella felt totally alone in the world. But she continued to remember her mother's promise that God would always be with her.

One day, a man who had heard that Isabella was a hard worker came to the tavern. At age 13, Isabella was growing straight and tall like her father. The man, John Dumont, offered to purchase the slave girl from the Schryvers for $300. To a struggling tavern keeper, that was a fortune. Isabella was sold once again.

The girl had been told that John Dumont was a decent man, but that his wife was difficult. Mrs. Dumont encouraged two hired white girls to make trouble for Isabella in the home. One of the girls named Katy did just that. After Isabella put potatoes on to boil each morning, Katy would sprinkle in a few wood ashes when no one was looking. Isabella received the blame for not properly washing the potatoes.

But the Dumonts' 10-year-old daughter, Gertrude, liked Isabella. By hiding and watching, Gertrude caught Katy putting the ashes in the pot of potatoes. Isabella had never had a white person stand up for her. This new revelation helped her understand that not all white people were cruel and unfeeling.

Because she had had so little teaching from any caring adult, Isabella thought her owner was some kind of god. She believed Dumont could actually read her thoughts. This kept her in constant fear, which drove her to work until she dropped from exhaustion. Dumont bragged that she could work as hard as any man.

While she pleased the master, the other slaves avoided Isabella because she made them look bad. One day, the Dumonts' driver took Isabella aside and explained to her that all her hard work would never set anyone free, it would just kill her sooner. He explained to her that Dumont was not a god and had no way of knowing her thoughts. This truth was especially freeing to Isabella. She could return to praying to her God in the sky.

It was about this time that Isabella met a young slave named Robert from a neighboring farm. Robert belonged to a man named Catlin, and thus he was known as "Catlin's Bob." The two may have met at the celebration of Pentecost. This holiday, known in Low Dutch as Pinkster, occurred seven weeks after Easter. Slaves from the area were allowed to come together and

Isabella's sweetheart, Robert, was beaten by his owner. Isabella and Robert were not allowed to marry each other. Instead they were forced to marry other slaves chosen by their owners.

celebrate with dancing, singing, and eating. Isabella might even have danced with Robert. We do know that Robert cared enough about Isabella to disobey his master.

Catlin did not want his male slaves marrying anyone but his own slaves. If Robert married

Isabella, any children they had would belong to Dumont, and Catlin would feel that he was cheated. Robert knew the rules, but he still stole away to see his lover in secret. One day, when Isabella was ill, Robert came to see her, but he did not know that his master had followed him. Watching from her window, Isabella saw Robert knocked to the ground and mercilessly beaten by Catlin and his two sons. There was nothing she could do to stop them. She blamed herself for Robert's beating and vowed she would never again try to see him.

In the end, Robert returned to the Catlin farm and married whomever he was told to marry. Isabella did the same, by marrying an older man named Thomas. Tom had already lost two wives who had been sold away from him. Although there was no real love between the two, Tom was kind to Isabella. They married in 1814. Isabella gave birth to four children who lived past infancy—Diana, Peter, Elizabeth, and Sophia. All, of course, were born into slavery.

In 1817, the New York State legislature passed a law. The new law said that all slaves born before 1799 would be freed in 1827. That meant Isabella would be free in 10 years. Ten years may have seemed like a long time, but it was much shorter than a life-time. Isabella began to count the days until she would be free.

As she patiently waited, Isabella continued to work as hard as ever. Not long after each child was born, she returned to the fields to work, hanging the baby's basket between two trees. When the infant cried, she stopped her work to nurse the baby, then returned to work again.

In 1825 John Dumont offered to release

A girl named Ellen was the daughter of one Georgia plantation owner and his slave. Even though her skin was fair, she was still a slave. At age 11, she was given as a gift to her own half-sister.

Ellen fell in love with another slave, William Craft. They secretly planned a daring escape. Ellen disguised herself as a man, and William pretended to be her slave. They safely traveled from Georgia to Philadelphia. Once there, abolitionists befriended them and invited them to tell their story.

Isabella, like this slave girl, had years of back-breaking work ahead of her. Instead of suffering, she decided to escape.

Isabella a year early if she worked hard. This news thrilled her, and she drove herself to work harder than ever. But when the moment came to receive her freedom, Dumont changed his mind. Pointing to her bandaged hand that she'd cut on a scythe, he accused her of losing a year of work because of the injury.

Isabella finally saw Dumont for what he truly was: a person untrue to his word. She knew she'd had enough. She decided that after she finished spinning the wool from the recent fall shearing, she would leave.

Afraid to leave at night and knowing she would be seen in the daytime, she prayed and asked God what she should do. The thought came to her to leave just before daybreak. She began to make preparations for her escape to freedom.

These runaway slaves faced a dangerous journey. Like Isabella, some were helped by Quakers or members of the Underground Railroad.

3

Exercising Freedom

Isabella's older children were now able to take care of themselves. Although she longed to take them with her, she knew Dumont and their father, Tom, would watch over them. Taking up baby Sophia and gathering her few belongings in a handkerchief, she set out down the road.

She did not know where she should go. When she stopped to feed the baby, she prayed for help and guidance. She thought of of Levi Rowe, a man who lived nearby. Knowing his kindness, she was sure he would help her. Rowe was on his deathbed and suggested that Isabella go to the home of Mr. Isaac S. Van Wagener.

Mr. and Mrs. Van Wagener were Quakers who did not believe in slavery. Once they heard Isabella's story, they gladly took her in. Within a few days, Dumont was on their doorstep. He accused Isabella of running away and demanded that she return with him. Isabella refused to obey him. Then Dumont ordered Isabella to give him Sophia. Again Isabella refused.

Mr. Van Wagener told Dumont that he would pay $20 for Isabella's freedom and $5 for the baby's. Since he did not believe in slavery, Mr. Van Wagener made it clear that he was not buying slaves. Rather he was purchasing Isabella's services until the end of the year. To Isabella's delight, Dumont accepted the offer. She was finally truly free!

Isabella thanked Mr. Van Wagener and called him "master." Mr. Van Wagener explained that he was not her master. He told Isabella to call him Isaac Van Wagener. This was strange indeed. Isabella was nearly 30, and she never had been without a white master over her.

Shortly before Isabella's escape, her son Peter had been sold to a friend of Dumont's named Dr. Gedney. Gedney planned to use the boy as a **valet** on a trip to England, but soon realized he was too young to handle the job. The doctor sold Peter to his brother, Solomon Gedney. Solomon soon sold Peter to his brother-in-law, a wealthy land owner in Alabama named Fowler. He did this even though it was against the law to sell slaves outside the state of New York. This was a law that few people obeyed.

When Isabella received word that her son had been sold into the Deep South, she was very upset. At the same time, something rose up inside of her. She'd seen her mother grieve over the loss of all her children. Isabella determined that the same thing would not happen to her.

Leaving Sophia in the care of the Van Wageners, Isabella walked to the Dumonts, where she confronted them about the sale of her son outside the state. With a tone of deep determination, Isabella informed Mrs. Dumont, "I'll have my child again."

She went to the home of Mrs. Gedney, the mother-in-law of Mr. Fowler. It was Mrs. Gedney's daughter, Eliza, who was married to Peter's new master. After listening to Isabella's sad story, Mrs. Gedney laughed at her.

Isabella then walked to Kingston, New York, where Quakers offered to help. Upon their advice she went to the courthouse and filed a legal complaint requiring Solomon Gedney to go to Alabama and bring Peter back. The Quakers also helped Isabella raise enough money to pay a lawyer to defend her rights.

It took many months, but at last the day came when Peter was to appear in court. Isabella was in for a shock. Peter cried and clung to his master, claiming that he did not know Isabella. Thankfully, the judge saw through the boy's act.

Asking to meet with Peter privately, the judge learned that the boy had been threatened with beatings if he did not lie as his master instructed. Because of the horrible beatings he'd received while in Fowler's possession, the boy was terrified.

In this courthouse in Kingston, New York, Isabella became the first black woman in America to win a legal case.

Isabella, the lawyer, and the court clerks finally convinced Peter that it was safe to tell the truth.

While it did not seem as important to her at the time as getting back her son, Isabella had become the first black woman in the United States to ever win a court case.

Isabella found a job for Peter at the river, helping to tend the locks. The locks were enclosures on the river with gates at each end used in raising or lowering boats as they pass from level to level.

As much as she longed to have all her family around her, it was impossible for her to do so. Even Tom was gone. After he was freed, Tom tried for a time to earn his own living. Soon he was forced to move into the poorhouse, where he died. Tom's situation was common among elderly slaves. When the white masters had worked their slaves nearly to death and had no further need for them, the slave owners would put them out with no care. Because these slaves knew nothing about tending a business or making a living, they quickly died.

During the time that Isabella spent with the Van Wageners, she often thought of friends and family she'd left behind at the Dumonts. The Van Wageners' home was very quiet and uneventful, and she missed the laughter and lively singing of the other slaves.

After a while Isabella got a feeling that Mr. Dumont was going to come and offer to take her back. She even told the Van Wageners that

Dumont would be coming. And she was right—he drove up soon after.

While she was preparing to dress Sophia and gather her things to go with Dumont, Isabella was supposedly stopped by a clear voice, which she knew came from God. She had a vision. "Who are you?" she cried out. The answer came to her distinctly, "It is Jesus." Suddenly she was flooded with peace and love. In later years, Isabella was surprised to learn that other Christians claimed that they had seen Jesus as well.

When she emerged from this vision-like trance, Dumont had gone. Isabella was never again tempted to return to her old life. From that moment forward, she never doubted that her prayers would be answered. The experience gave her great faith and boldness. Later, she often opened her speeches by saying, "Children, I speak to God and God speaks to me." Most people who witnessed her in action never questioned that fact.

After about a year of freedom, Isabella, Peter, and Sophia moved to Kingston, where Isabella

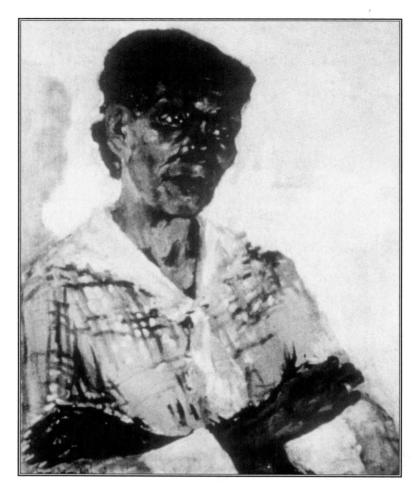

After Isabella was free, she worked as a maid, like this woman. Then she decided to move to New York City.

worked as a maid. She and Peter attended the local Methodist church with white people. While in Kingston, she met a schoolteacher from New

York City named Miss Grear. Miss Grear was taken with Peter because he was such a bright boy. Grear asked Isabella about Peter's schooling and about her plans for his future.

Isabella was surprised that a white woman was interested in her son. Miss Grear told her about a school in New York City that would accept Peter, and added that she would take care of the cost.

The fact that she could live anywhere she pleased was a new thought to Isabella. But it was one she liked. She thought about Miss Grear's invitation. While she liked the idea of Peter going to a good school, she knew they could not take young Sophia with them. There was only one solution: she would have to take Sophia back to the Dumonts' and ask her two older daughters, Diana and Elizabeth, to care for their little sister.

Once this was done, Isabella's mind was made up. She and Peter were ready to accompany Miss Grear to New York City.

This picture shows a busy New York City street in the 1830s. Isabella worked there for about 13 years before deciding to go east.

4

"The Spirit Calls Me"

New York City in 1829 was nothing like the busy metropolis it is today, but it was already extremely crowded for the time. Isabella and Peter had never seen so many people in one place. Boatloads of immigrants arrived at the docks daily, and thousands of New York residents lived in poverty.

Miss Grear helped Isabella find jobs doing housework for wealthy families. While she worked for several people, Isabella made her home with the family of Mr. James Latourette. Peter was enrolled in navigation school, where he would learn how to handle ships and chart their course by the stars.

In her new surroundings, Isabella looked for a church to attend. She first approached a church on John Street. Here she was told she was welcome, but she would have to attend services for "colored only." Isabella's anger boiled. Later, she located an all-black church, Mother Zion African Methodist Episcopal (AME) church. Established in 1787, the church was the oldest African-American organization in the country. Isabella found fellowship there, and she could worship any time she pleased.

While attending Zion church, Isabella was reunited with two of her siblings: her older brother Michael (the little boy taken from his parents in the sleigh all those years ago), and another older sister, Sophia. When they were first reunited, the three talked together for an entire day. Isabella asked about her sister Nancy and learned she had only recently died.

Meanwhile, a great "reform" movement was underway in New York during the early 1800s, and many women had become concerned for those less fortunate. By Miss Grear's invitation,

invitation, Isabella joined an **evangelists'** group that went into the poverty-stricken areas to preach. These areas, such as the one known as Five Points, were filled with crime, disease, and hopelessness.

Once Isabella saw the need there, she wanted to do more than just preach and sing a few hymns. She volunteered at the Magdalene Asylum, a shelter for homeless women. Located on Bowery Hill, the home was run by Elijah Pierson. While Pierson appeared to be religious, he was in truth an **impostor**.

Pierson impressed Isabella at first because he claimed to hear directly from God. Isabella had no trouble believing that, for she too heard directly from God. Pierson called himself "Elijah the Tishbite," a biblical Old Testament prophet. Isabella was innocent and eager to join forces with this man.

One day, while Isabella was working at the asylum, a man named Robert Matthews appeared at the front door. Although she didn't know it, Matthews and Pierson had a clever scheme to trick people out of their money. They started a community in Ossining, New York, known as "The Kingdom." Isabella believed what they said and joined their **commune**. She even gave away the small amount of money she had saved to help support their work.

As the only black person among them, Isabella did all the hard work and was excluded from the meetings. Just as she was beginning to see the error of her decision to join the group, Pierson suddenly died. The doctor said he had been poisoned, and Matthews was accused of the murder.

The court case became a source of gossip throughout the state. Newspapers carried story after story about the strange religious group. As the articles were read to Isabella, she was shocked to learn the truth about the commune.

One of the families who had been at the commune, the Folgers, would later cast suspicion on Isabella as the murderer, calling her a witch. They wrote a novel about the group, which **slandered** Isabella. Although she felt betrayed, by now

This is a portrait of Isabella. Everyone who met her respected her for her honesty and good character.

Isabella knew the power of the courts. With her usual determination, Isabella gathered character statements from those who had known her in the past. All whom she approached wrote letters vouching for her honesty and integrity. Even her present employer was convinced Isabella could never do such a thing. Eventually the court awarded her a sum of $125 to be paid by Folger for the damage caused to her good name.

While that problem was taken care of, another had taken its place. Peter was having a terrible time in the big city. He had dropped out of school and began running with a bad crowd of older boys. He turned to stealing to win their approval.

Each time Peter got in trouble with the police, his mother always bailed him out. And each time, he promised to do better. At last, Isabella realized she was doing him no favors. The next time he was arrested, she did nothing.

In desperation, Peter called for a man named Peter Williams, a local barber who was also a preacher. Williams made Peter agree that he would find work on a **whaler** and go to sea. Within a week Peter, now almost 18, had left aboard the *Zone of Nantucket.* Isabella was both happy and sad. She could only pray that this experience would straighten out her wayward son.

Although Isabella wrote Peter many times, a letter from Peter indicated he had not heard from her. The letter, dated September 19, 1841, was his last. Isabella never heard from Peter again, but she kept his letters always.

By 1843, Isabella had become somewhat disillusioned with New York City. She felt it was time to leave. During a time of prayer she received directions from God to go east, even though she'd never been east of New York and did not know anyone there.

An hour before she was ready to leave, Isabella informed her employer, Mrs. Whiting, that she was leaving. She added that her name was no longer Isabella, but was now Sojourner. Mrs. Whiting was surprised, asking, "What are you going east for?" The new Sojourner answered, "The Spirit calls me there, and I must go."

Sojourner always traveled very simply, as this photograph shows. She became well-known as an impressive speaker against slavery.

Becoming a Sojourner

Sojourner set out on her new journey in June 1843. Although she was about 46 at the time, she was strong and healthy with a keen, sharp mind. After taking the ferry to Brooklyn, she made her way out across Long Island. Even though she had just a few coins in her pocket, she was not looking for fortune but only opportunity.

To find shelter, she knocked on doors and offered to work in exchange for a place to sleep. When she found a church or camp meeting, she would rise to speak. This was known at the time as "testifying." Sojourner was a very powerful speaker. It wasn't long before her reputation grew and many people were talking about her.

She dressed in the drab colors of a Quaker woman with a white shawl about her straight shoulders. While appearing quiet and gentle, something powerful happened as she stepped up to speak. Sojourner held audiences spellbound, causing them to both laugh and cry.

She spoke about the evils of slavery and what it meant to live in such cruel treatment and absolute injustice. She told about her childhood, the pain of her beatings, and of losing her siblings as they were sold away. Her strong, clear voice sometimes broke out in beautiful song, some of which were of her own composition.

Soon, many newspapers were quoting her and more and more invitations came for her to speak. Traveling northward to Connecticut and Massachusetts, she eventually arrived in Northampton, Massachusetts. There she visited a cooperative community, one in which all members worked together and shared almost everything. The members of the community supported themselves by running a silkworm farm and making silk fabrics. They invited her to stay for a time.

After her bad experience with The Kingdom, Sojourner was quite wary at first. But she soon learned that this group was very different. The Northampton Association of Education and Industry, as it was known, provided a safe and friendly haven for leading **abolitionists**. Sojourner's stay at Northampton would change her life.

Many outspoken white abolitionists such as Wendell Phillips, Samuel Hill, Parker Pillsbury, and William Lloyd Garrison were frequent visitors there. Two black abolitionists, David Ruggles and Frederick Douglass, were also a part of the ongoing work. Sojourner was tremendously excited to hear open discussions on the topic of abolishing slavery. She listened intently and learned a great deal.

Garrison was the editor of an important

abolitionist newspaper, the *Liberator*, and he was also a trusted leader of the antislavery movement. Frederick Douglass was a very close friend of Garrison's. A runaway slave, Douglass was still a hunted man and could have been caught and sold back into slavery at any time. Parker Pillsbury from Michigan had suffered a great deal at the hands of angry **proslavery** mobs.

In addition to abolitionists, Sojourner also became aware of some of the leading women's rights activists of the day, such as Olive Gilbert. Gilbert would often read newspaper articles to Sojourner as they talked at length about women's rights. White women at the time were almost as helpless as slave women. They could

Susan B. Anthony was a school teacher from Massachusetts. She joined forces with Amelia Bloomer and Elizabeth Cady Stanton, campaigning for women's rights. She worked as an abolitionist and believed in a woman's right to vote. In 1872, she tested the law by voting in a presidential election. She was arrested and fined, but she refused to pay. The case was dropped. Unfortunately, Anthony did not live to see the legislation passed that gave women the right to vote in 1920.

Sojourner became friendly with William Lloyd Garrison (pictured here), who spoke out not only against slavery but also for women's rights.

not hold public office, serve on juries, or even hold down many of the jobs men did. More importantly, they could not vote, which kept

Sojourner was inspired by the example of Frederick Douglass, a great speaker and abolitionist.

them powerless to help change any of the laws.

Sojourner remained at Northampton for three years. The time she spent there became her training ground for the future. The courage of these men and women did much to convince Sojourner that she too could help bring about change for the better.

Because Frederick Douglass had written his biography, Olive Gilbert encouraged Sojourner to also write hers. William Lloyd Garrison even offered to write the introduction for her and print the books. So Sojourner dictated her many thoughts, ideas, and stories to Gilbert, who wrote the book.

The *Narrative of Sojourner Truth: A Northern Slave* went to press in 1850. This was the same year Congress passed the Fugitive Slave Act as part of the Compromise of 1850. The Fugitive Slave Act allowed federally appointed commissioners and marshals to seize runaway slaves and return them to their owners. Under this law, any person aiding a runaway slave was breaking the law and could face heavy fines or imprisonment. Signed into law by President Millard Fillmore, the Fugitive Slave Act fanned the flames of anger and unrest in the North.

No one person formally organized the Underground Railroad. It was a widespread secret network for aiding escaping slaves that slowly evolved over the years leading up to the Civil War. The following terms were used in its description:

passengers—escaping slaves

conductors—people who helped escaping slaves along the way

stations—places where people waited with food and clothing for escaping slaves

depot—a point where connections were made to further the journey

locomotives and cars—wagons, buggies, boats, or other modes of transportation to carry passengers from one point to another

When Sojourner's book came off the press, she was both pleased and excited. Olive Gilbert then gave her the bad news: no bookstore would carry the book. Store owners could not risk the mob violence of the proslavery movement. But that didn't stop Sojourner. She loaded a **carpetbag** full of books and took to the road to sell them herself.

She had found another way to support herself. Sojourner asked a traveling photographer to take her portrait. These photographs were printed up on cards with the caption: "I sell the shadow to support the substance." The photos depict her as a woman of dignity and grace.

In the years leading up to the war against slavery, Sojourner Truth traveled hundreds of miles, often on foot, to bring truth to people. She never allowed herself to be intimidated or put down. She often put **hecklers** to shame with her wise answers. Addressing her audiences as "children," and individuals as "honey," she displayed affection for all people whether they were friends or enemies. No matter what was discussed by speakers who came before her, she always turned the subject back to the cruelty of slavery.

While attending a Woman's Rights Convention in Akron, Ohio, Sojourner made remarks that would later make her famous. A preacher at the convention stated that women were weaker and needed to be lifted over ditches and helped into carriages. Sojourner replied, "Nobody e[v]er helps me into carriages or over mud-puddles, or gives me any best place. And ar'n't I a woman?"

She bared her arm to the shoulder showing the massive muscles from years of hard labor. "Look at my arm," she told the crowd. "I have plowed and planted and gathered into barns and no man could head me—and ar'n't I a woman?" Raising her voice still louder, she added, "Wh[ere] did your Christ come from? From God and a woman. Man had not[h]ing to do with him." Sojourner's remarks were answered by roars of applause.

Traveling took up almost all of Sojourner's time during the decade before the Civil War. Although she had bought a small home in Northampton, she almost never lived there. In 1857 she sold the property and purchased land in Michigan, near Battle Creek. Soon her daughter, Elizabeth Banks, and two grandsons, James and Sam, joined her there. Later, Diana and her husband Jacob Corbin came to live with Sojourner in Michigan as well. Sojourner's dream of having her family

This drawing shows Sojourner giving a lecture. She became famous for her speeches on women's issues and slavery.

around her came true at last.

Sojourner was in Battle Creek when the war broke out. At the time, she was in her

60s, but she was determined to do her part. After the government had agreed to organize black troops, 1,500 young black men joined the First Michigan Volunteer Infantry stationed at Detroit. After asking for donations of food and money to provide the boys with a Thanksgiving feast, Sojourner went to Camp Ward to deliver the large boxes. She talked with the solders, sang to them, and gave advice and comfort. Then she composed a song just for the Michigan Infantry.

Seeing all this war activity made Sojourner restless. Though she was far from battle, she kept informed of the news as her family read to her from the newspapers. She felt Abraham Lincoln was a great president, and she praised his action of setting the slaves free in 1863. In the spring of 1864, thinking the president might need encouragement, she decided to pay him a visit.

Taking her grandson Sammy, she began the journey. Along the way, Sojourner stopped and visited with old friends and gave speeches when invited. When they at last arrived in Washington, D.C., she learned it wasn't as easy as she'd thought it would be to visit the Great **Emancipator**.

In this painting Sojourner is with the "Great Emancipator," Abraham Lincoln. Meeting the president was a cherished memory of Sojourner's later life.

The End of
the Journey

Arriving in the capital in the fall of 1864, Sojourner and her grandson found themselves in the middle of a full-blown war center. The city's population had more than doubled in two years, and thousands of former slaves had taken refuge there. Rent was high and the muddy streets were bad. While the slaves were free, many business restrictions made it difficult for blacks to find jobs. The unhealthy conditions reminded Sojourner of the Five Points district of New York City.

Through contact with friends, Sojourner found her way to Freedman's Village, which had been set up by the army. The village was located in Arlington, Virginia, just outside of Washington. After she and Sammy had settled in, Sojourner quickly went to work.

Because most of the slave women had worked in the fields and lived with only the barest of necessities, they lacked basic living skills. Sojourner taught them how to sew, clean house, do laundry, comb their hair, and care for their children. She encouraged them to get an education and advance themselves. Knowing that they mistrusted white people, she told them that some white people she knew were good. Some had worked hard for the freedom of blacks.

After several months of hard work, Sojourner still had not visited with the president. Her goal was to talk to the president about the struggles of her people—to tell him that they needed more assistance than they were receiving. But when she finally entered the president's office, she saw the weariness on his face and changed her mind.

After a warm greeting, the president invited

Sojourner worked hard to help freed slaves like these find work and get an education in the North.

Sojourner to sit down. She explained to him that when he first took office, she expected him to be torn to pieces, but now she thought he was the best president who had ever come to office.

At the close of her visit, the president signed Sojourner's "Book of Life." This book was like an autograph book that she carried with her. The president wrote: "For Aunty Sojourner Truth, Oct. 29, 1864. A. Lincoln." His signature, along with many others, became treasured keepsakes in the later years of Sojourner's life.

After working at the Freedman's Village for nearly a year, Sojourner moved to the hospitals. She was often seen carrying large bags of supplies to help the sick and wounded. Because the walk was a long one and the bags were heavy, she often hailed a street car. The conductors, accustomed to ignoring blacks, would not stop for her.

After several encounters, including one in which her shoulder was painfully wrenched by a rude conductor, she decided to register a formal complaint. The president of the streetcar company told her to press charges against that particular conductor for assault and battery. She did as he suggested. As with her two former court cases, Sojourner won. The settlement caused a great stir in the city, and afterward all conductors stopped for blacks along the line. Her actions demonstrated to the freed slaves that they could insist on their rights.

After long months of work among her people, Sojourner came to the conclusion that freed slaves needed to leave the city. In her usual tireless manner, she made trips north to locate homes and jobs for them. Between 1865 and 1868, working both alone and with the Freedmen's Bureau, Sojourner helped between 3,000 and 5,000 former slaves find jobs outside of Washington.

While those numbers seem high, it was only a small part of what was needed. Sojourner's thoughts began to turn to the vast acres of land out west. She thought that because the slaves had unwillingly given years of unpaid labor, the government surely owed them something. There could be a land-grant program for freed slaves.

After a short rest back home in Battle Creek, Sojourner took to the road once again with Sammy by her side. This time she spoke out for her plan and gathered names for petitions to present to Congress. In 1870, on a trip back to Washington, she met with President Ulysses S. Grant. While the president was warm to her, it was clear that he had little interest in her land-grant plan. Sojourner then took her petition to Congress.

Most of the senators were not supportive. Only Senator Charles Sumner showed interest. He told her he would sponsor the bill if she drew up the petition and then gathered more signatures. Sojourner traveled as far west as Kansas seeking support, but when she returned to Washington a year later with hundreds of signatures, she learned that Senator Sumner had recently died. There was no one else who would help.

Discouraged, she returned home. Sammy had been ill during their travels. His fever and cough grew worse, and he died in February 1875 at age 24. Sammy had been like the son Sojourner had lost. They were close friends and travel companions. She mourned deeply over this tragic loss. Because she had very little money, she mortgaged her house to give Sammy a decent burial.

Grief-stricken, Sojourner told her friends that she was going home to Battle Creek to die. But

Sojourner retired to Battle Creek, Michigan (shown here). She finally lived with her family all around her, just as she had wished.

Sojourner still had nine more good years. During the early 1870s, upon learning of the terrors of the Ku Klux Klan, a white supremacy group in the South, and the nightmares of lynchings and mistreatment of blacks, she ventured out on one more lecture tour. This final trip took in 36 towns in her home state of Michigan. The year she turned 81, she was one of the Michigan delegates to the Woman's Rights Convention in Rochester.

At last Sojourner did slow down and was confined to her home, where her daughters Diana and Elizabeth, cared for her. When a visiting friend expressed sorrow over her condition, the aged woman said, "I'm not going to die, honey; I'm going home like a shooting star."

By late November, she was bedridden and very weak. Before she slipped into a coma, her last words were "Be a follower of the Lord Jesus." She died on November 26, 1883. The sojourner's journey on earth was complete.

Sojourner lived in Battle Creek the last 26 years of her life. In 1983, the citizens of Michigan inducted her into the Women's Hall of Fame in Lansing. The 200th anniversary of Sojourner's birth was celebrated in 1997. In September 1999, a 3,000-pound bronze sculpture of her was dedicated in the city.

The Sojourner Truth Institute of Battle Creek is located in the downtown area of the city. There, the historical society houses the most extensive archives of Sojourner Truth artifacts and records in the United States.

More than 1,000 people attended her funeral, and white men carried her coffin. She was buried in Battle Creek's Oak Hill Cemetery near her grandson Sammy.

All across the country, famous people paid their respects with glowing words. Newspapers carried articles about her life's work. The great abolitionist Parker Pillsbury summed it up best: "The wondrous experiences of that most remarkable woman would make a library . . . could they all be gathered and spread before the world." This is a fitting **epitaph** for a great American woman.

GLOSSARY

abolish–to end something

abolitionist–a person opposed to slavery in the United States

bondage–the condition of a slave; being under the power of another

carpetbag–a traveling bag originally made of carpet fabric

commune–a small community whose members have common interests and in which property is often shared

emancipator–a person who releases another from bondage; a nickname for Abraham Lincoln

epitaph–words in memory of a dead person, usually for a tomb

evangelist–a traveling preacher

heckler–a person who gives a speaker a hard time with questions

impostor–one who cheats others by pretending to be what he is not

Low Dutch–form of Dutch spoken by certain Dutch immigrants, particularly in New York and Pennsylvania

proslavery–in favor of keeping the slave system

slander–to make a false statement that harms a person's reputation

sleigh–an open, horse-drawn vehicle with runners for use on snow or ice

sojourner–one who travels, staying in one place only temporarily

valet–a male servant who performs personal services, such as taking care of clothes

whaler–a ship whose crew hunted and killed whales

CHRONOLOGY

1797   Born Isabella, a slave to Johannes Hardenbergh, in Hurley, New York.

1800   Hardenbergh dies; Hardenbergh's son, Charles, takes possession of Isabella.

1808   Charles dies; Isabella is sold to John Neely; her mother dies.

1809   Sold to Martin Schryver; her father dies.

1810   Sold to John Dumont.

1814   Dumont matches Isabella with a fellow slave, Thomas.

1826–27   Escapes from Dumont; stays with the Van Wageners who purchase her freedom.

1828–29   Presses charges and wins case to get son, Peter, back; moves to New York City.

1832   Joins a religious community, The Kingdom.

1843   Becomes a traveling preacher; changes her name to Sojourner Truth.

1847–50   Stays with the Northampton Association of Education and Industry in Northampton, Massachusetts

1850   Biography, *The Narrative of Sojourner Truth,* published.

1857   Moves to Battle Creek, Michigan.

1864   Meets with President Abraham Lincoln; joins the National Freedmen's Relief Association.

1869–71   Travels throughout the Midwest, gathering signatures on a petition asking government to give western lands to former slaves.

1883   Dies in Battle Creek, Michigan.

1983   Is inducted into the Women's Hall of Fame in Lansing, Michigan.

1997   The 200th anniversary of her birth is celebrated.

1999   A bronze sculpture of Sojourner Truth is erected in Battle Creek.

CIVIL WAR TIME LINE ═══════

1860   Abraham Lincoln is elected president of the United States on November 6. During the next few months, Southern states begin to break away from the Union.

1861   On April 12, the Confederates attack Fort Sumter, South Carolina, and the Civil War begins. Union forces are defeated in Virginia at the First Battle of Bull Run (First Manassas) on July 21 and withdraw to Washington, D.C.

1862   Robert E. Lee is placed in command of the main Confederate army in Virginia in June. Lee defeats the Army of the Potomac at the Second Battle of Bull Run (Second Manassas) in Virginia on August 29–30. On September 17, Union general George B. McClellan turns back Lee's first invasion of the North at Antietam Creek near Sharpsburg, Maryland. It is the bloodiest day of the war.

1863   On January 1, President Lincoln issues the Emancipation Proclamation, freeing slaves in Southern states. Between May 1–6, Lee wins an important victory at Chancellorsville, but key Southern commander Thomas J. "Stonewall" Jackson dies from wounds. In June, Union forces hold the city of Vicksburg, Mississippi, under siege. The people of Vicksburg surrender on July 4. Lee's second invasion of the North during July 1–3 is decisively turned back at Gettysburg, Pennsylvania.

1864   General Grant is made supreme Union commander on March 9. Following a series of costly battles, on June 19 Grant successfully encircles Lee's troops in Petersburg, Virginia. A siege of the town lasts nearly a year. Union general William Sherman captures Atlanta on September 2 and begins the "March to the Sea," a campaign of destruction across Georgia and South Carolina. On November 8, Abraham Lincoln wins reelection as president.

1865   On April 2, Petersburg, Virginia, falls to the Union. Lee attempts to reach Confederate forces in North Carolina but is gradually surrounded by Union troops. Lee surrenders to Grant on April 9 at Appomattox, Virginia, ending the war. Abraham Lincoln is assassinated by John Wilkes Booth on April 14.

FURTHER READING

Chang, Ina. *Separate Battle: Women and the Civil War*. New York: Puffin, 1996.

Collier, Christopher, and James Lincoln. *The Civil War: 1860–1865 (The Drama of American History)*. New York: Benchmark Books, 2000.

Lutz, Norma Jean. *The Rebel Spy*. Urichsville, Ohio: Barbour Publishing, 1998.

Mettzger, Zak. *Reconstruction: After the Civil War*. New York: Lodestar Books Dutton, 1994.

Rinaldi, Ann. *Amelia's War*. New York: Scholastic, 1999.

Sinnott, Susan. *Charley Waters Goes to Gettysburg*. Brookfield, Conn.: Millbrook Press, 2000.

INDEX

PICTURE CREDITS

page

ABOUT THE AUTHOR

NORMA JEAN LUTZ, who lives in Tulsa, Oklahoma, has been writing professionally since 1977. She is the author of more than 250 short stories and articles as well as more than 40 books, both fiction and nonfiction. Of all the writing she does, she most enjoys writing children's books.

Senior Consulting Editor **ARTHUR M. SCHLESINGER, JR.** is the leading American historian of our time. He won the Pulitzer Prize for his book *The Age of Jackson* (1945), and again for *A Thousand Days* (1965). This chronicle of the Kennedy Administration also won a National Book Award. He has written many other books, including a multi-volume series, *The Age of Roosevelt*. Professor Schlesinger is the Albert Schweitzer Professor of the Humanities at the City University of New York, and has been involved in several other Chelsea House projects, including the COLONIAL LEADERS series of biographies on the most prominent figures of early American history.